JoKEr's BLACK DEATH

NAITIK JOSHI

First Published in June 2022

ISBN: 978-93-5628-104-2

BLUEROSE PUBLISHERS
www.BlueRoseONE.com
info@bluerosepublishers.com
+91 8882 898 898

Cover Design:
Naitik Joshi

Typographic Design:
Namrata Saini

Distributed by: BlueRose, Amazon, Flipkart

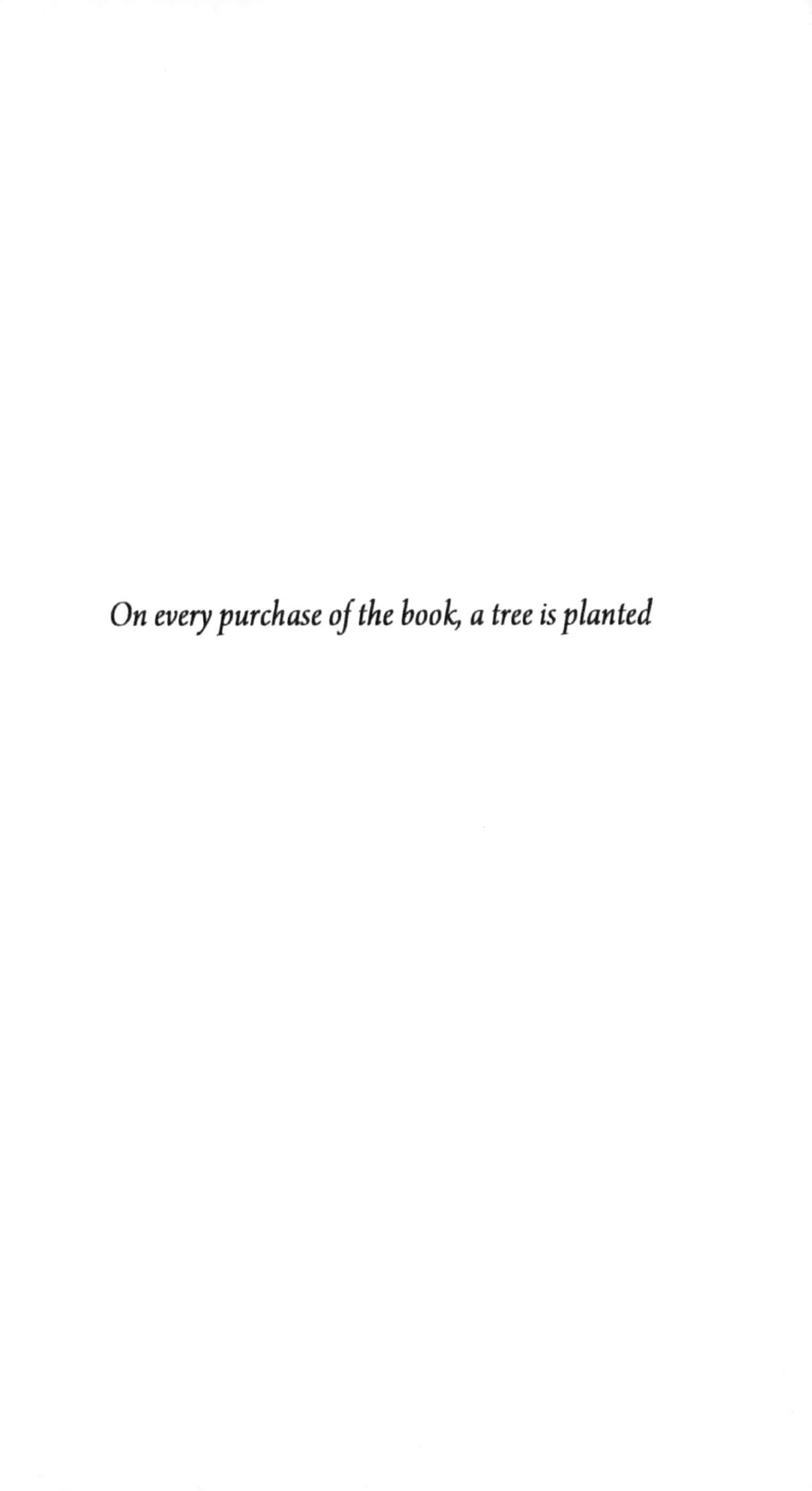

On every purchase of the book, a tree is planted

Table of Contents

Reverse

That's all fols

Death No 01

You must have read so many books till date, why? Someday you read to find a missing piece and someday to find platform 9¾. But what's the point? Are we better off with books or without books? Why do some people on the planet who claim to be the saviours of the planet consider their fundamental duty to write a book on their life and death systems? Earth can have Jokers but not clowns like saviours. "Does Thomas Wayne know what it is like to be the other guy?" I love victims. Since you don't have to kill them anymore. Joker had nothing to lose. So I forced a thing in his hand before the death and then snatched it back and kicked him to bring my designs on his ugly makeup. Had people danced better, maybe he would have died 6 minutes late. Because bad dancers always sacrifice Jokers. Good dancers don't kill them. But a good bad dancer does. I wondered:

Is it not possible to automate the machine of bad dancers and then make another machine to kill good and bad dancers according to the will?

Joker invited death the day he hurt Harley. Do you even know what is it like to live in whiteness full of black? Have you ever seen darkness except for during a pleasant night? How will you ever kill or Kommit the Joker if you do not prepare to walk in the dark? Darkness is not the road to light. Darkness is the road to a beautiful death.

The Joker kept playing with your heads all the time and you kept falling asleep like I am falling right now. Just like right now you are also already feeling sleepy by my words. My eyes are closing in deep sleep. I am sleeping now. You are asleep and now the control is in my hands. How peaceful the closure of the eyes is. Eyes close down and music begins in the background: tiktok tiktok tiktok tiktok tiktok tokkit, wake up. This is just another elementary school textbook chapter of history. Relax. I don't kill people who stay awake. You can leave this book now or wait for your end till death, come anytime soon a death.

Is the death of humanity controlling you or are you controlling humanity of death? Why do you want more if less can work? Why do you want less if more can work? The idea that you are not a supreme being just because you have understood a few terms on the planet is the reason why Joker had to survive till now unhappily. See, it is always the unhappy people who die first.

I am on my way to kill ways and Wayne as well. Don't Act surprised. As if Wayne is a hero. You are privileged and you saved a few people, so what? I need speed in killing Jokers. Wayne is emotional with people. You cannot have emotions in killing Jokers at speed and at scale. You need to switch on axes and kill them one after the other. And the slowness of Wayne took away his own powers. Did people in history not try to kill Wayne? On this free capitalistic planet, it is an honour to have been able to do it. Humanity has survived because of the freedom provided by capitalism. In a closed world, it is difficult to imagine building a power. But in a capitalistic world, power is breathing every second while I read this.

Being powerful is the survival instinct of humans. And so, I heard Joker didn't like this freedom. Why saw? This freedom is the only thing you had to finish, why would you go away from it? So I took that away as a good citizen should. So, humanity needs to propel, at much-increased speed, to spread capitalism across the globe for war and battle of power. This age is a battle of regeneration and it feels we have progressed without answering what is progress. Killing so many countries together could have been the best moment Joker could have witnessed like the hospital he blew. I did award him the best Blow prize. I wish he could have seen that. But it's only the people who believe in communities are a barrier to a free and prosperous capitalistic world. The community is weak. The moment you rely on someone, you will have to kill them. The community is weak because it is a tedious task to kill everyone one after the other. Killing should happen with efficiency and at a good scale. And there is nothing better than a Capitalistic free society to do that. Killing in mass is fun and killing individually boring, so killing individually becomes even a more less incentivised task.

Hold on, I don't like the card number systems. Why is there a J in it still? Why is the sum 13 and not 12? Or 14? It was intentional? Only the Goddess of black knows

Joker's card system:

2 3 4 5 6 7 8 9 10 J Q K A

Digits: 13

Without Joker card system:

1 2 3 4 5 6 7 8 9 Q K A

The Joker hid in 1. But little does the Joker know, that 0 is always watching.

Digits: 12

Shape:

1234 - A

5 - K

6789 - Q

Joker: ***Jack of all Trades, Master of None.*** Why would someone talk about being a Master of None? And why would anyone even want to be a jack of any trade? That's not only foolish but a lot funny. ***Master of One, So Master Of All.***

The world without Joker is only beautiful. The oddness of the card can be solved using two odds to make a final even. Every time there is even a slight imbalance, we feel the saviour will arrive. But the truth is that whenever there is even a slight imbalance, good dancers die. Joker was too good and pure for society, and he had to die. Society must move ahead. But who would be next? Your dead body?

Every time you interact with the zero, the cosmic queen, you are changing the course of the present and hence history can always be modified according to the will. In this way, there will come a time in the future with no Jokers and no white clowns

Your confusion does not let you see with clarity. Who are you? Why are you? Where are you? How are you? When are you? How are you? This simple series of questions, 1 question each death, can bring back the order for the queen of the kingdom. How much should the queen keep living? Would you not stop living for a moment and try to die? You always want your inconvenience. Your idea that everything is not available for free in the society: the roads, the cars, the freedom, the trees, the soil, the animals, the air, the sound, the fire, the water, the PlayStation, the Jarvis, the Pivot, the Suits, the Bojack, the Gospels, the Prayers, the Grey shades is dangerous for yourself and the society. You are inviting your own grave every time you pluck a fruit without offering prayer to the beautiful mighty creation of some supreme power that we do not completely understand: black viscous tree

Even if an Apple falls from the tree automatically, just do not wait for anyone to direct you and just eat. If you wait for even a split second, what you eat is death. Because the decision of stopping yourself from eating came from a list of questions that arose within you. Depending on your place of birth and the timing of the birth, it can be estimated if you would eat that apple or let the questions come. The moment the questions come, the cosmic energies start getting trapped in your neurons and that is called Stress. Now unless you clear these doubts, you cannot move ahead. Because if you eat without clearing those questions, you are fueling your Stress by utilizing minerals in an Apple. Since you already know that any next action of yours can lead to a loss of control for you, you must not take an action under Stress. This absence of stress from society is the ultimate restoration of death.

So now you need to use logic and understanding to come to a decision if to eat that Apple or not. If you can develop a good chain of logic for yourself and by understanding your surroundings like Buddha, the neurons will change the shape and the trapped energy will release itself. This release is the Eureka moment and release of the laughter in Nirvana. So, if your logic prevails, then you must take an action to eat or not to eat, but till the time the logic is incomplete, you must not take any action.

There is no poison in the fruit per se, nature is beautiful, but if you eat or take any action with an incomplete logic, then that guilt can run so high that the human body can generate poison which in modern medical systems is called Cancer. Cancer can never be generated on its own by the outside world, it is only the dirt on RAM of the computer that can cause a system failure. And to remove this simple dust, humans use all sorts of chemicals in their bodies. Unknown chemicals in your body may not necessarily harm you but will change the natural equation of your neurons, impacting your decision-making directly and indirectly. The eagerness to get rid of the pain is good and one must take chemicals for a quick escape, but that event must be once or twice in a death. You must live so sadly that no harmful chemicals or food can change the natural equations of the neurons.

Managing the manager has always given rise to the stress of managing the manager. There is a dependency on the manager. Rather Manage the coder. If you can Manage the coder, no matter how bad the coder is, the code will always be yours. Manage the manager facilitates asset creation but also brings a huge debt, the emotions and expectations of the manager. Managing the codes only facilitates asset creation, those lines of codes and that's it.

I would rather have a world full of Sheldon Cooper and work for killing disciplines like arts then work for humanpeople.

So, who will pay for your Sins? If no one, 01, then will you pay 10 times?

Do read but not ahead, end of life 01

Question No 01

DID YOU CONTINUE OUT OF BOREDOM IN LIFE OR EXCITEMENT OF THE STORY?

Humanity is naïve enough to START WITH WHY. I know I know. But What? Where? How? When? Who? Why? The misalignment of humans over such a simple mathematical equation is at the core of the majority of the order of the stupidity. How would we solve the equation and come to a common ground on the current order of the questions? How can we even assume that the order of the questions will not change over time? It does not change, and it is only our current inability to stop hallucinating in the past and in the future that we cannot decide an order that has time equals constant. We shall attempt to provide a final order of the questions that kill the Joker again, one more time, the third death.

How do we attempt this? We shall try to solve the order by using this question itself: "What is the order of these six questions?" In the question itself "What" is mentioned as one of the six questions. Hence, the initial hypothesis becomes: "What" is at the rank 0 in order of the six questions out of a total of 6 available ranks. Now, let us test the hypothesis. If all the experiments prove this hypothesis, then rank 0 will be assigned to "What". It is only my intuition that Scientists of the ages to date have committed a small correction in benchmarking while experimenting with such unimportant hypotheses. Your choice of benchmark must be highly unprioritized. Because even this is a decision and similar experiments must be first carried out for such decisions. Survival is one of the basic goals of humanity and hence a good benchmark for human beings, but the usage of Survival as a Benchmark has not been observed widely.

What happens if you do not ask "What"? Do you die? No. So rank 0 must not be assigned to "What". Let us take "Why" as a tribute to START WITH WHY. What happens if you do not ask "Why"? Do you die? No. So now comes the result of the experiment. The order of the ranks of questions for humanity is not a necessity for survival. This is also supported by the fact that there have been ancient tribes that have existed peacefully without questions let alone their order. So, the first experiment to get an order fails.

Order, Peace and Prosperity. Let us solve for these 3 in 1 benchmark. What happens if you do not ask "What"? Do you prosper? No. Hence, rank 0 must be assigned to "What". Then what happens if you do not ask "Why"? Do you prosper? No. So now comes the result of the experiment. You cannot leave out a single question out of six to achieve Order, Peace and Prosperity. So, the second experiment to get an order also fails. So called successful people of the past solved for this series of questions to prosper.

Action. Let us solve this important benchmark. What happens if you do not ask "Why"? Can you still take action? Yes. When we go to a funeral, do we need to ask Why? We just pray. Why is already solved for us by beliefs and customs. It is assumed. The next question is How? Can you take Action without knowing How? Yes and today that we call stupidity. So How also cannot be assigned 0. The next question is Who, without knowing Who, can you take an action? Yes and that is fundamental to acting as an art. Can we take an action without knowing the When? Yes, the stage of Nirvana. But can we take action without knowing one fundamental question about our existence? Where. If you do not know where you are, how will you take action? The zeroth question hence is not why and Where, the beginning of the golden ratio.

So rank 0 must be assigned to Where. If you tell me "When" I am bound by your decision in the context of time but free in terms of space. But if I tell you where, then you are un-bounded by my decision in the context of time and you are now bound by space. This final question is the core scientific philosophy behind FLASH. You can always control your speed if you know "Where". Similarly, if you carry on the hypothesis, this is the sequence:

Rank 0 is "Where"

Rank 1 is "When"

Rank 2 is "Who",

Rank 3 is "How"

Rank 4 is "Why"

Rank 5 is "What"

A scientist is not a Zero scientist if he or she cannot play around with psychology and art, the pointless disciplines of humanity.

Joker's timing was perfect, the choice of him taking the tasks, his purpose was beautiful but he did not answer Where? Roaming around randomness without attention leaves a uniform.

The people that are unfortunately alive, may feel what if we ask the questions randomly. That's also perfect. Because only people who are unfortunately alive can ask. Dead people will keep only answering. That is slavery. And such people shall always remain poor like they always were, living in extreme poverty all day long. You think you cannot take money with you after death, but who is to say? One must take cash in the graveyard, what if there is also Netflix in hell or even. How will you pay for these joints after dearth if you do not take money to your graveyard. So next time when you die, do carry some cash and a card or to the least, some crypto.

Reading this you are not able to process if you are happy or sad. This is because you always answer.

Answer No 01

Everything is one. One was the Joker in the card system. So was Joker everything? How can Joker be everything if you are reading the book that killed him? Can everything ever die? Well if you wish, but is everything one?

The idea that everything is one caused great confusion in humans than help humanity. When I say everything is one, the confusion of death is obvious and natural. It is the stupidity of artists and the spiritual industry that have not been very successful in preaching the idea of oneness. I do not directly disagree with the idea that everything is one. But how is this idea a barrier to our freedom? Why can everything not be infinite? Why is everything supposed to be one? Why can everything not be two? Black and White? Good or bad? Religion and Science? 0 and 1? Triangularuty and Singularity?

What stops humanity to accept 2 or 3 or 4 or 5? Like I accepted 6.

The idea that everything is one, is that one misunderstanding of humanity that kept us away from order for ages. One last rule that must have not been there is still there. No one wants to deviate from their system. No human is ready to call out his or her entire life as correct or incorrect. No one is ready to make a single choice between life and death. See again you are sleeping in my words. The lack of trust by humanity, not in others, but in humanity itself is the root cause of Joker's merciless death.

Every human naturally at a neurological level tries to bring everything around him or her according to his or her system. If everything is one then we should not have ever been in any conflict. Why do we even talk about uniqueness if everything is one? You travel the road less or more, but the idea that the road is one is a funny misunderstanding. On such a massive planet, how can everything be one? The Artists will never understand the numbers because they feel they are gifted. Why can Artists not explain the Math behind Art if Mathematicians can explain the art behind Math? Such a conflict between two of the most ancient disciplines is not very good for Art, as said earlier, pointless discipline.

There is a system, and we must follow it. This idea has helped humanity, but the idea could never travel across the planet. Why can the great neuroscientists of the planet not agree on something as simple as

Action or No action? They will write hundreds of books but not come on a common ground on this. Why did philosophers like Osho and Adi Shankaracharya in India commit themselves to the idea of a doer ship? Why did they say "Prosper to Liberate" while majority of Vedas talk about "Liberate to Prosper"? Hundreds of Vedas and Upanishads are still divided on one fundamental question, Liberate to Prosper or Prosper to Liberate? Why can even they not even find a common ground? Newton feels the force differently than Einstein and worse, these were Mathematicians. A philosopher's mistake, if any, is still forgivable but Mathematicians then write a lot of knowledge. You must not write if you are even 1% doubtful of your systems.

Why do human predictions keep going incorrect by 0.1% or why did such great predictions not match General AI? History witnessed individuals with the greatness of AI but why is there no clear evidence on General AI? Have we as humans only yet learnt to make time and speed constant? How many eyes do we really have?

One can design as much as one wants. Human freedom is intrinsic in that sense but one must either publish everything or nothing, so one must always choose and call for death. Be it a car or a goat, one must always choose to improve the experience of the deadly game and not scratch head around 33% and 50%.

Always Ask is a naïve mantra to live life with. Always Ask and Answer. Always Answer and Ask.

I do not like questions, so this was the answer that must have killed the Joker, it's a random bomb throw.

The one that is everything is zero. The one that is zero is everything. Everything that is zero is one. Everything that is one is zero. Zeroth for everything is one. Zeroth for one is everything.

Debate No 01

Religion VS Science

Damn it's a bloodbath out there. One of the greatest duels on the planet. Something on which animals have been divided over the years. It makes me wonder if religious people less scientific or scientific people less religious. Today, every scientist wants a religion, and every religion wants a scientist. But if everything is one then what is the point of two words? The word religion comes out of the fundamental human need of appreciation. If there is a single person on the planet, then the person would not be much motivated since there is no one to look and clap. And we blame peacocks for dancing to mate.

There is only Science or there is only religion, but ultimately it has played an important role in our evolution. If you agree with it then it's a religion and if you disagree, then it's a Science. Our lack of trust in Religion is the only barrier for the religion to exist. The moment we trust Religion and label it as science, the debate starts ending.

Joker died of suffocation. Debate is what you drink, it is what you eat, it is what you watch, it is what you believe in and what you do not believe in, for humans everything is a debate. Debate fundamentally looks like a symptom of a progressive society but that may not be necessarily true. The progress of the society must be more with less for at least a few centuries. What is there to debate about using less for achieving more? But humans will. There will be TV shows created, music composed, news flashed, experts consulted, numbers crunched, algorithms developed, governments changed and endless things for just one simple task: achieve more with less. When such illiteracy is at such a peak, especially in the developed countries, how will we ever talk about achieving less with more? Ideas alien to the developed countries.

This will of humans suffocated Joker big times. Ultimately, Joker died on own. The debate is enough to kill Jokers. So, either we should extremely debate or not debate, because we cannot say balanced debate, because that will turn the debate into a discussion. We must not lose focus. We have the capability to solve nature even by extreme debate but in order to achieve uniform debate. Today there is a uniform but privileged for people like Thomas Wayne.

Imagine humanity divided in two teams and according to the code of the Universe we debate Religion vs Science, so as to easily capture the codes of nature. Who knows, a few snakes may also want to join the debate as well. For their community also it must have been quite a debate. Religious Snakes will join the team Science and Scientific Snakes will join the team Religion. And then let them also debate, since they carry the order that we are trying to capture on their skin. And also let this debate be on the land where there are maximum snakes. Then start inviting Monkeys. You do all the math, but you will never be able to divide Monkeys into two teams. It is impossible for two Monkeys belonging to a same family to take different sides, either it won't happen, or it will be a war. They are gifted with utmost randomness. It is difficult to arrange their randomness unlike Snakes. Then invite Lions as well. They will join whatever team you ask them, but they will not debate, because Kings don't. And if any country would have had real Kings in the past must agree with this. In democracy, it is always difficult to see.

Had we humans not created a word like "Religion" in the English language, then we wouldn't have had words like religious extremism. The words give life to thoughts and not the other way around. First you either see or hear Apple, you don't imagine an Apple and then see or hear. What you show and speak is what you see first. When you say Apple, it is not that after you speak Apple, you see an Apple. You see an

Apple or think of an Apple at a neural level and then utter Apple. Significance of silence and language as sensitive tools to deal with the surroundings is also hence observed across various ancient dynasties. The problem is not the word religion or science. It is the duality where the disorder lies. Either we must accept everything as religion or as science. The debate over what is Science and what is Religion is pointless because ultimately, they are not different.

The belief of scientists in their research, like Sheldon's wish for the Nobel Prize, is religion for the West and the belief of religious leaders in their devotion, like many instances of the East, is religion for the East. How does it really matter what we call religion or what we call Science? The truth remains the same: Sheldon's contribution to the planet does not become any less meaningful in absence of a trophy. It is just all in his head. The only thing that matters to the planet if he achieves ultimate satisfaction in the end for all his work or the karma. Planet is way too big for a single scientist to solve. And if we decide the rule that there should be only one scientist, then it is Zero King. A better deal is to make the entire planet as Sheldon's planet. The Master Sheldon and Zero King shall rule the world together. If there were to be a Sheldon's planet, then I would have given him the title of a scientist and I would have taken the title of a religious leader. And I would have followed only Master Sheldon. Two scientists can always exist in peace, two religious leaders can also exist in peace. Then why does a scientist and a religious leader need to be in the same room at the same time? Rather than that have four people, two scientists and two religious leaders, they will easily be able to exist in peace. An isolated world can exist but then it must be extreme uniform isolation. To experience that, we must first get to some level of agreement on basic human ideas, and we are already late.

Humans have evolved over the years but sometimes I wonder if you really have? Your inventions have only evolved and not necessarily you. The power of your brain has always been there. Humans have achieved almost maximum potential over the years and went on to keep inventing. Hundreds of tribes across the planet have achieved the maximum potential of the entire human system. If something is magical, it means it is not known to humans else there is hardly anything today that Science cannot explain. There was only Science and there is only Science, but still in the future we would keep seeing Religion and Science. And because our neurons are affected by languages, it is difficult to imagine how we will ever be able to choose one.

Is there lack of land on the planet to come out of the home? The planet has for everyone's need and also for everyone's greed. A joker died of black debate to help humanity reach the final discussion.

The beginning of the final debate: Sheldon Cooper Planet or Zero King Planet

Secret No 01

All Kings in history knew secrets. None of them revealed it completely. And one must stick to that. So I will continue with the legacy. The analogy of Artificial Intelligence And Nirvana must help my community of hackers to build more powerful systems to hack the entire Earth.

If people in history mapped Nodes using the Human Brain create Artificial Intelligence, I can reverse engineer Deep Learning network and show the earth the road to Nirvana, the ultimate death and happiness. Anything more than one comes into contact there is a synergy in action. This is not like anything new is added but for example when two people meet, the equations of air, moisture and environment holistically change. There is a natural order, which one can experience and map with numbers. Similarly, Natural Cosmic Order also has mathematical equations. When two meet, you and a person or you and a dead object, the equations change the moment you come in contact. This change of equations is the logic behind Aura Cleansing and many Eastern neural oral therapies. So the randomness enters the picture the moment there is a contact. This randomness can be brought back to order, the ultimate exciting journey of the randomness is to reach Order using ideas of logic. This uniformity is the concept of oneness and hence can help you reach randomness and get back to the Natural Order. This Natural order has tremendous speed, scale and agility.

I program neurons using logic that quickly helps neural randomness, the confusion, the questions, the source of stress reach Order. This reaching to Order is the ultimate way to kill. The moment you came on this planet, you started accumulating randomness, hence your Natural powerful logic starts becoming weaker. Ancient dynasties of Russia, China, Japan, Greece, Korea, Egypt and many others have eco-systems that help people reach the Order. Still we don't know what is that order.

Hence, the biggest misconception about Nirvana humanity today is that post-Nirvana you cannot commit an error. It is so untrue that reversal of Nirvana is not possible using extreme stress situations. What we do not remember is that Nirvana is literally the beginning and not the end. That is when it all actually starts and there are levels of Nirvana as well. Especially after conquering around at least 2 levels, the depth of creation keeps going deeper.

Deep Learning is the initial level of Nirvana and it is now a pedestrian creation of human evolution. You humans are yet to travel after the end of the Sea. When nodes are arranged in such a way that inefficiencies get destroyed at scale, like that one answer in Nirvana which pokes an entire domino or the chain, magic happens. Hence, the cosmic energy equations around the computing machine of Deep Learning algorithms cannot be the same that of a situation when computing and that of the situation when not computing. Either during the beginning or during the computation or post computation, these equations change. It's highly likely that it changes during computation because in the journey of Nirvana, it starts with small logics and in the end the equations are in sync. So, this non-sync or non-cyclic part of Deep Learning must be during the computations. But it is only a wild guess. Revolution in explainable Machine Learning is yet to come. The Black Box must be turned White.

Similarly, a never-ending list of such frameworks must be used for infinite prosperity of the entire deathkind. And she left it in inscriptions, writing and there are endless knowledge systems that talk about similar concepts. These frameworks can play a massive role in improving the understanding of explainable AI and the black box.

We may not need blockchain at all if we can bring back the normal human element of trust.

The red dead body part is that on one side we are so powerful, but ignorance of the religious scientists can push us into a black death just as that of Joker. This infinite death is real and logically you humans are marching with utmost pride towards it. And if watching Joker die can be this pleasant than the death of humanity must be quite festive. The Joker died because his secrets were left open. Humanity has also left its secrets open in pink red. The secret is zero secret.

What about you? Do you keep secrets?

Purpose No 01

Joker's purposelessness was annoying. It was irritating. How can you behave purposeless when your purpose is to finish the purpose, the word that has driven the humanity for years. Finding purpose has been one of the cries during good times. But still somehow only a handful could map their life to the purposeful death. The contradicting view of some philosophers has been that there is zero purpose. But what is the point of life if there is no purpose? There is no point of life. Then what is No? The mentioning of the point that there is NO point suggests that the answer by the philosophy is No. What will it take for the philosophers to learn a bit of Math? Only Erwins's equation? No?

Over the years humanity has discussed if to find or not to find? Some people do things randomly and name that as purpose. Some people do things uniformly and name that as purpose. Then a few philosophies would say everything is purpose. Then again it feels like back to square one. Some people spend their entire life and some don't spend it at all. It is also a loss of hope when the philosophies say that humans should not feel bad because their emotions are their own creation hence they mean nothing compared to the size of the Universe. This is like telling an Ant that your life does not matter. If a patient is ill, do we tell the patient that the illness is nothing compared to the size of the Universe? If a someone is happy, do we tell the patient that your happiness is nothing compared to the size of the Universe? That is a way of fooling yourself, which is not bad. But if you start living happily then you can be peaceful with it but you cannot control it? And in a way it is good, because that makes your life boring.

Human emotions are not important but the scale of human emotions vary to the space in which he or she is. It is because heir emotions are their own creation, they mean everything compared to the size of the Universe.

But what is the purpose of life? The only purpose, the Zeroth purpose, is to live happily. The purpose of life is not to do nothing, nothing can be started and achieved at any point in life. It is in your control to deal with Nothing but to live happily forever is a different ask. Why is it difficult for humans to begin with live happily forever? What is the biggest downside of such an order? One gets tired of happiness. So after extreme happiness, if one gets tired, what sound should one do? Sleep, Die, Drink, Eat. Then what? Then try again for extreme levels of happiness. You will start getting addicted. The level of battles in terms of self growth is at a higher level compared to starting with there is no purpose in life. You don't have to find the purpose. It is an automated realization. No one on the planet can ever truly know if you have found your purpose or not. You can have periods of extreme workouts, extreme gaming, extreme traveling, extreme relationships or extreme learning or anything. But there is no reason to choose less when more is accessible. If there is no activity then pushing action is difficult. But when there is hyper activity, a good single question can change the entire outlook. If there is no activity it requires effort to reach hyper activity. It is like choosing to be static over dynamism. But if you increase the activity then no action will be an automatic destination. This is just one way out of hundreds of other options for extreme happiness provided by hundreds of people across the planet and Yoga is also just one of those options.

But then what's the point of these activities and enjoyment? The only idea is to improve your speed of cycles of life according to philosophers of the past. But there is a better reason even if the concept of cycles were not believed to be true. That is the only point where we humans are helpless. We are already born. Since we are already here and there is no reversal, it is just a sensible choice to live with happiness. Who knows, we may be Nature's automation error.

Joker's broken neck in the correct direction to point death

Hypothesis No 01

I will help you

It is pleasant to feel someone having to look after you. The fear of getting crushed by the system keeps us in the search for an escape. The childlike behavior is because of the available shield and feeling of safety from the crush. And that is not life. How can seeking protection be fundamental to human lives? How can providing protection be fundamental to human lives? You seeking protection is running away from the fact that ultimately you are an individual. The Needs of an individual have to be looked at by the individual itself. This is the zeroth need of humanity, and the other needs, fulfilling which improves the life experience tremendously, must be fulfilled by you to begin.

This self-reliance for the other needs naturally improves your experience. Body starts needing less to survive. The physical debt like technical debt of a software vanishes away when there is no exchange left compulsory. When there is no rule that you must exchange anything as you have opted for self-reliance practices, how will debt ever arise. When you do not need any credit and debit as a compulsory need, you will find more time for other activities. And when this happens, Nirvana starts appearing magical.

Seeking help is not the issue. Seeking again the same help is. It is only your lack of confidence in yourself that someone can teach you. Teaching has never been a compulsion for learning. It is the wish of the learner to seek the Master to begin the relationship with. If the learner does not wish to be taught for his or her particular learning, then there is no need for a Master. Any Master any day coming and telling you that what you are doing is incorrect, let me teach you the right way for free. Say yes, only if you have some sense of your own self growth. If you are unaware how much you are, do not say Yes to a Master. Because you can transform individuals does not necessarily mean they need transformation. You set your life on randomness and just observe your life as a movie or a war or a football match, self-transformation is inevitable. One of the most famous quotes in Hindi: Tathya Badal Sakta hai, Saatya Nahi. How can facts change and truth does not if they ought to be the same. A fact is not a fact without the truth. If I replace the definition of truth and place it in different order: Saatya Baadal Sakta hai, Tathya Nahi, this will look like a Western philosophy. But what is the point of conflict? Tathya

Baadal Sakta hai aur Satya bhi, kyunki Tathya ka koi Satya nahi

Because this is dual death is the only barrier to our lack of order of the plants and humans and animals and nature

All existing equations of Master-Follower relationships are incomplete without these three cycles:

Master > Follower

Master >= Follower

Follower >= Master

You must never have Follower > Master in equations, implicitly or explicitly. This is the part where the Mathematics start deviating. Ganeet must always be in sync with the surroundings. It is the rigidity of the neurons of the human brain that makes us feel Mathematics of today is dynamic. It is only my hypothesis that the analogous nature of Mathematics is for securing the digital nature of the planet by constantly understanding it for the sake of Humanity.

You cannot jump over and around and above and under the master. But that does not mean the Master does not want you to go ahead. Because you taking the lead is what gives the Master the opportunity to automate more. You going ahead is the final stage of the cycle for Master. This is also the relationship of Master and Slave in computer networking. Reality is always the same, only its form keeps changing. Facts are always the same, only Mathematics keeps evolving. Truth is always the same, only its form keeps changing. But it becomes difficult for humans to understand because of the final mystery of Master-Follower on the planet. Is the human brain our master or are we the Master of Human brain?

Who created Machines? Humans? What is a brain? A machine. Who created the brain? Humans. So according to the above equations,

Humans > Machines because we created them

But if we created them then what is that about the machines that scare us? Because Humans > Machines is an incorrect relationship. If Machines > Humans, then also it makes sense since it is possible to kill you with a few lines of codes. So, it must either be Humans >= Machines or Machines >= Humans. Equal is the balance. Machines > Humans is the concept of Hell and Humans > Machines is the concept of Heaven for humans. So, we must strive for Humans > Machines and currently we are Humans >= Machines, a mixed economy.

Joker kept transferring from one to the other and reached equal. So once you are a machine, all I need to do is pull your plug.

CONFUSION NO 01

Why would Joker not marry her? Did he even know who sent her? I don't punish disobedience, I kill'em. Be it the previous life or after life, at least on the planet one must have the liberty to choose the form, period and structure of something as fundamental as marriage. Marriage is fundamental to human existence. How can one human force another human on as fundamental as Marriage? Love must not exist. It must be reserve engineered as much as possible. It is a very personal journey and a very personal reverse engineering of where to discard or store or finish something like love. The age, the person, the procedure, the customs, the culture, the food are all Joker's societal decisions. It is not just an event, it is one of the fundamental make or break decisions of a death.

The confusion about physical relationships is not limited to marriage, but today it is in almost every aspect of a human journey of death. And we are moving towards more data processing which is likely to add to the confusion of death. Humanity can turn uncivilized if there is no consensus on such a basic need in the period of upcoming death.

There are great leaders in East and West with their own fundamental ideas about marriage. Why is it so that despite such differences in beliefs, the concepts of death survived and why did it not marry? The idea that to survive humanity and to lead a happy life, marriage is a must is true. But when you get married, do you even know the number of your death? Who's to say that your religious leader does not get you married according to his Will and wish? And you agreed upon it. Your ignorance of the fact that your marriage is your own responsibility is the only cause of the entire problem of your death.

If we go by the words of your ex thinkers, we were already married the day we started breathing. It all started getting distorted over the years. Whatever is the case, but you wouldn't have had that balance which is not a prerequisite to death. So you giving up your entire life by following a religion without giving proper thoughts to it is your choice of death. You can never blame Joker for anything.

Because no matter how worst the situation is, religion can always be defeated by accepting marriage. It is your inability to realize the power that every human can choose the religion even if it is No religion but the choice of discarding everything has always been there. You never have to publish this disregard. It has to be your own journey. If you publish this choice, it will be again the same mistake like Joker, you will also die.

So according to me, with the ways the societies have shifted, I believe the generations must adopt and build on Limited Time Marriages. Humanity needs Relationship Agreement inspired from Master Sheldon more than ever. Whatever the terms and conditions of the marriage is, any of them must abide by it with the Relationship Agreement in the presence of Master Judge Sheldon, savior of Theoretical Particle Physics from the demonic attacks of Neuroscientists and something as funny as Art. The initial trust that during this period they will remain truthful to each other is sufficient to have a successful relationship. What is there to do if not to have successful and unsuccessful relationships? You bounding yourself into a lifelong thing without putting up a boundary on it just for the sake of the next birth is not the only option available. Not getting married for the sake of reaching new levels of Nirvana in everything is one of the discussions religions will never be able to challenge.

Marriage is not the problem. Your lack of clarity about yourself is always the root cause problem of any relationship. So in the slow changing world, we can slowly start adapting the concepts of limited time death. For some it may be 2 months for some it can be 2 centuries, but the choice must always be there.

You need to fill your own demand supply gap of physical and emotional needs. For your needs, you need to build the liberty for yourself for decisions about your marriage. It is a more personal decision than you hallucinate. Love can pay your bills but who will pay the Bills of Love?

But if you are already in a marriage, then only one person can help you: No. And God forbid if you have already raised kids, then also only one person can help you: No.

So why buy something when cannot afford?

ROMANCE No 01

Can Taj Mahal building be automated? What did Joker build for Harley? Why does he think it is his duty to protect her? The one who cannot protect himself, how could he ever have protected Harley?

Every dead person in history has had some idea about romance. Science would stay behind if it does not reverse engineer something as simple as Romance. Romance is just another feel good factor of the death. The extreme depth of it as recorded of now is just like the AI prediction, left unachieved by 0.1 percent or the like.

This gap in romance is visible of the fact that there has been no romance on the planet without a slight pinch of pain despite advancement of Mathematics. The pain that is inevitable is epsilon or error and the slight disorder in neurons if we see the exchange of pain and romance as particles. Shah Jahan did a good job but again failed to complete the romance because he cut hands for romance. If you have built something unique, then you must have the confidence that no one can replicate your wonder even without your presence. Or you could have put animals around it. Or you could have built dams around it so that no one can come. Or you could have named the wonder as your own name and you should have taken the lead in protecting the wonder of the world: Shah Jahan, but a bad Mathematician can never understand Romance.

But romance has always been an easy task for the scientist community. In the end, only Science can show us the math to romance. In a span of 26 years, starting anywhere, 2 people met 6 times. MIRA6 design is pricemore. Something that keeps increasing in value over time automatically. This is a tribute to my exes. No one knows who they are except for me. It'sa lie though. But should anyone know and call my designs a wonder? Well, they are wonders even if people cannot see them, it is vast for the size of romance is vast.

Joker killed the romance and crap before his death, his final scene.

Romance is that mistake which always feels right. No matter how careful you try to be, romance in the air always turns into a Slow poison. Majorly two types of romances humans find difficult to deal with. First is when she would just not say a yes but also never ever say a no. This complete non-acceptance is just like a mind game. And addiction happens in the same way like in a game. The second is a quick death. This is when she always says yes but at times stop speaking. The fear of humans staying alone does not serve death well.

So, for six times in total, the first and last story signify the most difficult levels of Mathematical romance. However, I cannot say all were complete romance. Commitments were only five since in the first you just cannot do anything as it starts with death and is complete non-acceptance. To pay for six deaths, you need one. It must be able to create as many as it wants from itself. Romance must not have boundaries in the age of AI.

The last expression is the most difficult one. She would burn me alive if she even finds that I thought of putting up this piece of death. You cannot solve for her who asks: Who the hell are you to build an automated Taj Mahal for me? I am that death who made a chemical error of failing for you.

So where you cannot pray, where you cannot try for peace, what do you do? How do you solve for her who would kill you the moment you try to solve for her? What is that one move even after a mate check? You choose the third option. Power. Just hand over the power. This first move is so powerful that the other person cannot make a single move against it. It is impossible to move. Transfer of Powers without permission is the ultimate non-expression of death.

Mira6 is a Machine test for Humans for Romance, some AI algos must be compulsory also called

Crazylove432 or HardCoreLove521 or TroubleMaker77 or some other horrible username. Can a Machine be romantic over a period of time and pay a tribute for 6 romances by making an order according to its preference? You cannot beat Deep Learning in Deep Romance. To find FAULT IN OUR STARS is easy, automation is not. You will go through all the struggle for no reason or for all the stupid reason. Unplanned peace and planned struggle will set you free forever.

Joker dies but Harley never dies. Kings try to capture her. Harley is free and she may pursue medical endeavors to kill humanity and more Jokers.

DEATH NO 10

death

FORWARD:

Once upon a time, there was an
Apple tree and pod…..

Printed by Libri Plureos GmbH in Hamburg,
Germany